Dave the Brave

A Division of The McGraw·Hill Companies

Columbus, Ohio

www.sra4kids.com

SRA/McGraw-Hill
A Division of The **McGraw·Hill** Companies

Copyright © 2002 by SRA/McGraw-Hill.

Printed in the United States of America.

Send all inquiries to:
SRA/McGraw-Hill
8787 Orion Place
Columbus, OH 43240-4027

ISBN 0-07-569968-0
    3 4 5 6 7 8 9 DBH 05 04 03 02

"I am the bravest!" Dave said. "Today, I swam across a lake to save a dog."

"But, Dave," said his little sister, Val, "you can't swim."

"I came face-to-face with a big cat in Africa," said Dave.

"But, Dave," said Val, "you are scared of cats."

4

"I saved a snake from a dragon,"
said Dave.
"But, Dave," said Val, "you hate snakes."

"I raced a truck on a dirt trail," said Dave.
"But, Dave," said Val, "you can't race."

Just then a big snake came up to
Dave and Val.

"I'm afraid of snakes!" said Dave.

"Scram, snake, scram!" yelled Val.
She chased the snake.

"You're brave, Val," said Dave.
"Yes, Dave," said Val, "but will I
ever be as brave as you?"